Quarters

By Mary Hill

Children's Press®
A Division of Scholastic Inc.
New York / Toronto / London / Auckland / Sydney
Mexico City / New Delhi / Hong Kong
Danbury, Connecticut

Photo Credits: Cover and pp. 9, 11 © Photodisc/Getty Images; p. 5 © H.D. Thoreau/Corbis; p. 7 © Klaus Guldbrandsen/Science Photo Library; pp. 13, 15, 17, 19, 21 by Maura B. McConnell
Contributing Editor: Shira Laskin
Book Design: Mindy Liu

Library of Congress Cataloging-in-Publication Data

Hill, Mary, 1977–
    Quarters / by Mary Hill.
    p. cm. — (Money matters)
    Includes index.
    ISBN 0-516-25058-2 (lib. bdg.) — ISBN 0-516-25173-2 (pbk.)
    1. Quarter-dollar—Juvenile literature. I. Title.

CJ1835.H555 2005
737.4973—dc22

                                                2004007189

5 6 7 8 9 10 R 12 11 10 09 08

Contents

Quarters are **coins**.

Coins are a kind of money made of **metal**.

Quarters are made of **nickel** and **copper**.

nickel

copper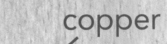

George Washington is on
the front of the quarter.

He was the first president
of the United States
of America.

UNITED STATES OF AMERICA

IN GOD WE TRUST

LIBERTY

S

QUARTER DOLLAR

9

Some quarters have a bald eagle on their backs.

The bald eagle stands for **strength**.

11

There are also quarters that honor each state in the United States of America.

These quarters have different pictures on their backs.

13

Many people like to **collect** these state quarters.

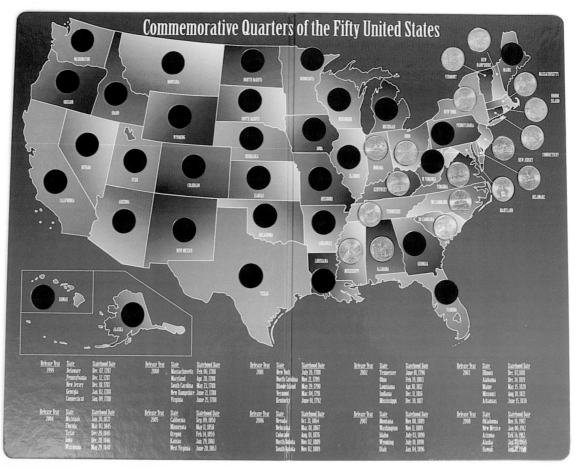

Commemorative Quarters of the Fifty United States

Release Year	State	Statehood Date
1999	Delaware	Dec. 07, 1787
	Pennsylvania	Dec. 12, 1787
	New Jersey	Dec. 18, 1787
	Georgia	Jan. 02, 1788
	Connecticut	Jan. 09, 1788

Release Year	State	Statehood Date
2000	Massachusetts	Feb. 06, 1788
	Maryland	Apr. 28, 1788
	South Carolina	May 23, 1788
	New Hampshire	June 21, 1788
	Virginia	June 25, 1788

Release Year	State	Statehood Date
2001	New York	July 26, 1788
	North Carolina	Nov. 21, 1789
	Rhode Island	May 29, 1790
	Vermont	Mar. 04, 1791
	Kentucky	June 01, 1792

Release Year	State	Statehood Date
2002	Tennessee	June 01, 1796
	Ohio	Feb. 19, 1803
	Louisiana	Apr. 30, 1812
	Indiana	Dec. 11, 1816
	Mississippi	Dec. 10, 1817

Release Year	State	Statehood Date
2003	Illinois	Dec. 03, 1818
	Alabama	Dec. 14, 1819
	Maine	Mar. 15, 1820
	Missouri	Aug. 10, 1821
	Arkansas	June 15, 1836

Release Year	State	Statehood Date
2004	Michigan	Jan. 26, 1837
	Florida	Mar. 03, 1845
	Texas	Dec. 29, 1845
	Iowa	Dec. 28, 1846
	Wisconsin	May 29, 1848

Release Year	State	Statehood Date
2005	California	Sep. 09, 1850
	Minnesota	May 11, 1858
	Oregon	Feb. 14, 1859
	Kansas	Jan. 29, 1861
	West Virginia	June 20, 1863

Release Year	State	Statehood Date
2006	Nevada	Oct. 31, 1864
	Nebraska	Mar. 01, 1867
	Colorado	Aug. 01, 1876
	North Dakota	Nov. 02, 1889
	South Dakota	Nov. 02, 1889

Release Year	State	Statehood Date
2007	Montana	Nov. 08, 1889
	Washington	Nov. 11, 1889
	Idaho	July 03, 1890
	Wyoming	July 10, 1890
	Utah	Jan. 04, 1896

Release Year	State	Statehood Date
2008	Oklahoma	Nov. 16, 1907
	New Mexico	Jan. 06, 1912
	Arizona	Feb. 14, 1912
	Alaska	July 03, 1959
	Hawaii	Aug. 21, 1959

A quarter is worth twenty-five **pennies**.

Four quarters make a **dollar**.

19

Quarters can be used to buy things from **machines**.

People use quarters to pay for many things.

New Words

coins (**koinz**) pieces of metal with pictures and numbers on them that are used as money, such as pennies, nickels, dimes, and quarters

collect (kuh-**lekt**) to put things together in one place

copper (**kop**-ur) a reddish-brown metal

dollar (**dahl**-uhr) an amount of money equal to one hundred pennies or four quarters

machines (muh-**sheenz**) things that are made to do work or to help make other things

metal (**met**-l) a hard material that comes from the ground and is used to make many things, such as coins

nickel (nik-**uhl**) a hard, silver-gray metal

pennies (**pen**-eez) small metal coins that are reddish-brown in color, and are each worth one cent

quarters (**kwort**-uhrz) coins that are equal to twenty-five pennies

strength (**strenth**) the quality of being strong or having power

To Find Out More

Books
Coin Collecting for Kids
by Steve Otfinoski
Innovative Kids

Money
by Sara Pistoia
The Child's World, Inc.

Web Site
The U.S. Mint's Site for Kids
http://www.usmint.gov/kids/
Learn about making coins and play games on the United
States Mint's Web site for kids.

Index

About the Author

Mary Hill is a children's book author. She has written books about many different subjects.

Reading Consultants

Kris Flynn, Coordinator, Small School District Literacy, The San Diego County Office of Education

Shelly Forys, Certified Reading Recovery Specialist, W.J. Zahnow Elementary School, Waterloo, IL

Paulette Mansell, Certified Reading Recovery Specialist, and Early Literacy Consultant, TX